Sarna's Big Dream

GAURI SUBRAMANIAN

Illustrations by Mira Subramanian

To all Dreamers...

~ *Chapter* 1~

It was evening time. Sarna was looking at the sun setting behind a distant hill. Her best friends, Tilly and Mukul were there too. They would play this game where they pretend to be each other's neighbors and invite each other to their imaginary home, cook together, and have fun. A mound of rocks would be the stove, half a coconut shell, the pot in which they 'cooked' the food, which would be anything they could find around the forest floor.

Tilly made a coconut shell filled with some seeds, pretty flowers and gave it to Sarna, and said, "I made you a special dish for your birthday!"

Mukul clapped and asked Sarna: "How old are you now?".

Sarna laughingly said, "I'm seven, just like you".

Mukul, "Oh, it's going to get dark very soon."

Tilly got up and dusted herself off, "I think we should get going. My mother told me to come home before dusk."

Mukul asked Sarna, "Let's go. Aren't you going to go home?"

Sarna, "I'll stay a bit longer to see the sunset."

Tilly smiled, "You see it every day. How is it going to be any different this time?"

Sarna, "You guys go. I'll leave in a bit."

Tilli and Mukul left. Sarna watches as the setting sun casts a glow on her surroundings. She is not afraid of the forest. This is her home. In fact, her parents have told her that in the forest, and in the mountains, lived their god Mahanguru.

The sun was setting behind the mountains. The trees and rocks were casting long, unusual shadows. Some of the shadows looked like animals.

Some of them even looked like her friends, Tilly and Mukul! She made shadow puppets with her hands for a bit. Soon she thought, *enough playing with the shadows.* She needed to get home soon because tomorrow was a special day! Tomorrow, she will be going to school for the first time! Not everyone gets to go to school. Her friends, Tilly and Mukul, are not going. Tilly's mother wanted her to learn how to do household chores, and she had overheard Mukul's mother saying "There's no point in these kids going to school. It's better for them to spend that time learning valuable skills like gathering firewood, cooking, cleaning, etc. Isn't it?" Sarna's mom often overheard women of her village say these things. But her mother never said these things to her. Sarna's mom, Alaka, was an artist who knitted clothes. She would weave beautiful designs on Sarna's dresses. She would make small, knitted costumes for the bamboo-wood dolls Sarna's father would create and sell during festival season in the city. Sarna's father was named Nemil. He was a farmer and artisan. Every time she came back from the main city, he would bring books for Sarna. Those books would have pictures and stories that he read to her. Sarna loved when her father read to her. Sarna adored her parents. They were both such good artists, and she looked forward to learning their skills once she grew up.

Sarna reached home. Her mother was waiting for her.

Sarna asks, "What have you made today?"

Sarna's mother answers, "Dal mandi."

Sarna says happily, "Dal mandi! Did you make it with spinach?"

Sarna's mother answers, "Yes. Now go get yourself clean and come for dinner."

Sarna quickly went to the bathroom to wash the twigs and dirt off herself and joined everybody for dinner. Dinner was so good! She loved dal mandi. She finished the dish quickly.

Her mother says, "What's the hurry Sarna?"

Her father asks," Yeah, why is the birthday girl in such a rush?"

Sarna says, "Mother, father, don't you remember? Tomorrow, I'm going to school! I have so many things to pack! I don't want to miss school tomorrow!"

Sarna's mom smiled, "Don't worry! I'll wake you up on time."

Father smiled and said," Wake me up as well, I have to go with her too."

~ *Chapter 2* ~

Next morning, the sun seemed to shine even brighter than usual. The scent of jasmine was in the air. Sarna put on her best clothes and took her cotton bag that her mother stitched for her. It was white, decorated with colorful flowers. She put her notebook in her bag with a sharpened pencil. She was all ready to head out to school.

School was a forty-minute walk from Sarna's home. It was the only school in her village. She walked with her father as he told her stories of the forest and mountain gods. They walked on a thin dirt pathway, both sides of which were tall *Sal* trees. She always felt so tiny in comparison to them. As they walked, the forest ended, and the rice paddies started. They crossed the rice paddies and reached the river. The river had a rope bridge which they crossed. Then, Sarna reached her school. The school was peach colored, with brick red paint on its columns. There were so many other girls just like Sarna! It was the first day for all of them. They gave Sarna a blue uniform. She sat on the classroom floor with all the other girls. The teacher came and started writing on the black painted wall. Sarna was in heaven. This was the most exciting day of her life! She was missing her friends Tilli and Mukul. *It would have been so much fun if they were here*, she thought. The teacher clapped and said, "May I have your attention?" snapping Sarna out of her thoughts. She turned to pay attention to the teacher.

~ *Chapter 3* ~

Soon, Sarna was in fifth grade. Books were her favorite thing. They took her to another world, where she otherwise couldn't go. They answered all her curiosities and questions. But lately, there was one question that was bothering her. No book was able to find the answer for her. The question that she was bothered by was what she would do after her fifth grade. There are no more grades after fifth grade. This is the only school in her village. Tilly and Mukul would sometimes tease her that after fifth grade was done, she would get married, and so she should learn how to cook and do household chores. Even though they were just joking, Sarna would still get panicked sometimes just thinking about it. Her entire world revolved around books and her passion to learn. She wanted to go to school and learn more.

It was Children's Day at their school. The school celebrated by students performing a folk dance and then singing their national anthem. They also invited a local politician who was standing for the upcoming election as chief guest. Sarna had heard from her father about politicians. He had told her that they were very powerful. If they wished, they could bring electricity, water, and roads to their village. But more than water or electricity, Sarna wished to go to school. She had prayed to her god, Mahanguru, many times for this. But it is believed that Mahanguru grants your requests by sending an opportunity or someone to help you achieve it. For Children's Day, all the kids dressed up nicely. They sang the national anthem. The students who were outstanding in sports and academics were handed trophies by the chief guest, the politician. Sarna won an academic award, since she was good in studies. She got to see the politician up close, and it felt, for a moment, that he was the person that Mahanguru sent to help her. After the trophies were distributed, the politician, Mr. Chougule, held a speech. He said that he was a servant of the people, and he would help their village. Sarna's eyes lit up. *He's the help I was looking for!* After the speech ended, Mr. Chougule asked, "Does anyone have any questions?" Sarna jumped and raised her hand. Mr. Chougule pointed towards her and spoke. "What would you like, little girl?" She says, "I want to go to school and study more, but there are no more grades in our school. What should I do?" He smiled, glancing around the room. He could feel the eyes of everyone on him, waiting for an answer. *I can't just brush off this one.* He said, "If you are really interested, you can join the school in the main city." Then someone asked him, "But it's too far, do we have to travel to the main city every day?" Mr. Chougule replied, "If you get admission, you'll have to live in a hostel." He looked towards Sarna. "Would that be alright?" Sarna couldn't answer his question. She was quiet. She never thought of leaving her parents. "You don't have to answer now. Let me know tomorrow, so I can put in a good word for you." He smiled. After the ceremony ended, everyone headed back home. Sarna also went back to her house. She had a huge dilemma. She thought, *I've never been to the main city. I don't want to go! I don't want to leave my parents!* She reached home and told everything to her mother. She started to sob. Her mother said, "Come here, dear." and patted her lap. Sarna came and sat on her lap. "I know you love us, and don't want to leave us. But you also want to go to school, don't you? This is a good opportunity. Take it! If you really love us, you should follow your dreams and join the school. You can always come back once you've finished your studies." She points at her dad and says, "And your dad will visit you too! There's no need to worry." Her dad came close to her and gave her a small doll made of bamboo wood. He said, "This is for you, dear. Always keep this with you. She will be your best friend. If any kind of problem bothers you, ask her. She knows all the answers." Sarna felt comforted. But it was a difficult choice to make. She had to choose between the comfort of her house or going to the new school and staying in a hostel.

Next day, after thinking hard, Sarna made a choice. She went to school and walked to the principal's office. Mr. Chougule was sitting there, chatting with the principal. He saw Sarna and recognized her. "You're that girl! Have you made up your mind? Do you want to go to the main city?" Sarna says, "Yes." The politician's eyes widened slightly, looking a bit taken aback. *Did she decide to leave her village for her studies?*

He replied in an even tone, "Okay, if you're really sure, then ask your parents to meet me tomorrow in the principal's office." Sarna said, "Okay!" and went back to her classroom.

Next day, Sarna's dad went to school to meet the politician. He told Sarna's father to head to the main city, and he gave the address and asked him to meet the new school's principal to get her enrolled. Sarna's dad went to the main city the next day and got her enrolled in the school. The school was a girls-only school. It was run by the local government, and free of cost. They had free accommodations for their students as well. Now finally, Sarna was all set for going to a new school! It all felt so surreal to Sarna. A few days ago, she was panicking about the likelihood of her getting married and saying goodbye to having an education. And now, she was actually going to further her studies. She thought, *If I would have gotten nervous and never asked the question, or if I would have chosen to stay home, this day would never come. All this happened because I chose to take the first step!*

~ *Chapter 4* ~

Today Sarna was leaving for the main city, to join the new school. She had mixed emotions. She was very happy about going to school in the main city, but at the same time she was sad since she wouldn't be able to see her parents as often. She would miss her friends, her home, and her forest.

She had packed her bags. She placed the bamboo doll crafted by her father in the bag, and then she headed to the bus stop with her parents, which led to the train station. While they were waiting for the bus, she looked at her mother and tears sprang to her eyes. Sarna realized this was the last time she'd see her mother for a while. Mukul was there with her father, Mani.

Mani asks, "Hope you've packed everything necessary. Did you pack rice and water?"

"Yes." Nemil replies.

Mani says, "Sarna will be the first girl from our village to head out for studies."

Nemil responds, "Yes, she wanted to study more and the school in our village is too small."

"No offense, but I don't understand. What is the need of taking such a big step? It's too risky, and the main city isn't safe. How will she manage on her own?" Mani says while frowning.

Nemil answers, "Don't worry, I've figured out all the arrangements."

"But I don't get the point. After all, she will be taking care of her family when she grows up. What's the use of this?"

"She wants to go to school and learn more. Why should I stop her from doing what she likes? I'll be happy if she's happy."

Just then, Tilly came running with her mother. "Oh my God! I'm so glad the bus hasn't left yet." Sarna hugged her friends. She wished that they could also come with her.

Her father was accompanying her on her journey. Soon the bus came, and they were on their way to the train station, and finally to the main city. It took them several hours to reach the main city. It was a long, tiring journey. They got out of the train and left the train station. The main city looked very different. It felt as if they'd come very far from their village. There was no forest. Instead, there were a lot of shiny vehicles, buildings, and people hurrying about. The dirt road was replaced by wide concrete roads. The *Sal* trees were replaced by tall concrete buildings. There was too much noise. It was too much for Sarna to handle. She gripped her father's hand.

They took a taxi, which took them to a huge building, surrounded by walls and a large gate. There was a guard at the gate. Sarna's dad introduced himself and Sarna, after which the guard allowed them to pass. Inside the gate, there was a long walkway leading to the building. There were gardens on both sides of the walkway with beautiful flowers. Birds chirped and butterflies lazily fluttered around. It was like a small forest within the chaos of the city. Sarna felt a bit more at home.

Sarna and her dad went to the principal's office, located on the upper floor of the building. Her father introduced her and himself to the principal. She was a nice lady. She welcomed them and offered a tour of the school. As Sarna walked through the hallways, she investigated the classrooms. *These classrooms had chairs and tables.* One of the classrooms also had computers. *I've only read about them in books!* There were many other girls, all watching the new student curiously. The principal introduced her to her class teacher. "Sarna, this is your new class teacher. Her name is Ms. Kalani." Sarna looked at her, and then at her sweater. *Her sweater is so cute! It looks hand knitted.*

Ms. Kalani asks, "So, you're the new student! What's your name?"

Sarna replies "It's Sarna."

"Nice to meet you, Sarna. Welcome to your new school! How do you like it so far?" Ms. Kalani says in a kind tone.

"I like it! It's very big."

Sarna looked at Ms. Kalani, shyly pointing at her sweater, "Your sweater is so beautiful!"

"You like it? I knitted it myself! Thank you, Sarna!"

Sarna remembered her mother. She was also an amazing knitter. Sarna liked her teacher a lot.

Her father says, "Okay, Sarna. Now you go with Ms. Kalani. She'll show you your classroom and your dormitory."

"But Father, aren't you coming too?"

"No, dear. I have to go back now, or I'll miss the evening train."

Ms. Kalani assures, "Don't worry, Sarna. I'm here for any worries you may have. Go say your goodbyes and come with me."

Sarna looked at her dad with teary eyes and hugged him. She then waved him goodbye and followed Ms. Kalani.

Ms. Kalani took her to another building that was close to the school building, where the students stayed. She showed Sarna her dormitory room, where she would be staying along with five other girls.

They all had a bed, a shelf, a table, and a portion of the wall they could decorate. Ms. Kalani said, "This is your space. Now relax and unpack your things. Dinner's at 6:30, in the first-floor hall. I hope to see you there!" Then she left. Sarna sat on the bed. Everything felt so new. She was nervous. *This is the place where I'm going to stay from now onwards.* She looked around the room and saw what other girls had put on their walls. She got to unpacking her own stuff. She took out her bamboo doll and put it on her shelf. As she took out her books, she heard footsteps. Some girls, around Sarna's age, entered the room. They gathered around her bed like bumblebees around a flower, chattering to each other. One of the girls asks, "Are you the new girl?" Sarna replies, "Yes." The girl continues, "What's your name?" "It's Sarna." The girl looks at the book she was holding in her hands. She asks, "Is this your book?" "Yes." Another girl pipes up, "That's the one written by Sarojini, right?" She says, pushing up her glasses. "Yeah, she's my favorite poet." Sarna says. The girl smiles, "She's my favorite too!" They both say simultaneously. "We're studying her books next class." the one with the glasses says. "By the way, my name's Vinya." All the other girls then introduced themselves, one by one, and invited her for dinner. Sarna felt much more relaxed. She was glad she'd made some new friends.

~ *Chapter 5* ~

Her school had girls coming from different backgrounds. Some had always lived in the city, some from other villages, but Sarna was the only one from a forest village. She used to tell her friends stories about her home and her forest. She was a great storyteller. Her friends were always enchanted by her tales. Sarna valued her relationship with her friends a lot. She made lots of friends very quickly and was always complimented on being honest and helpful. But she also happened to meet people who tried to take advantage of her kind nature. Sarna tried her best to always surround herself with good friends and brushed off negative experiences. Whenever she felt especially gloomy, she'd talk to her bamboo doll for comfort. She had seen her parents being strong, doing the things they believed were right when the world was against them. She never forgot how strong they were, and she tried to be strong just like them.

There was an upcoming event in her school, a festival. There were dance programs, plays, music etc. Sarna was just going there to have fun, though. She was a bit scared of dancing or acting in front of a crowd.

Instead, she was helping backstage, organizing, and making decorations for the event. After school, she went to her room. Suddenly, she heard soft sobs. She realizes that it was Vinya. With a concerned voice, Sarna asks, "What happened? Why are you crying?"

Vinya replies, "You know the upcoming dance performance? I'm performing with Sumi, but she fell ill! She has a high fever and won't be able to dance with me. We had been practicing for this for so long! I was really looking forward to this. I can't dance alone! What should I do? Everything is ruined!"

Sarna says, "I'm so sorry, Vinya. But I have an idea to help."

Vinya looked at her, "How?"

"I can be your partner in the dance."

"Can you dance?"

"I'm not that great, but I can learn from you!"

Vinya smiled and hugged Sarna. She says, "Okay, there's two days left. Let's practice after school, and I'll show you the steps. Just follow my lead!"

They practiced together. Sarna got the hang of the steps. Soon, it was the day of the festival. Everyone was getting ready, putting on dresses and makeup. *They looked so pretty!* Sarna was dressed up too.

She had never dressed up like this before and felt rather conscious. She was incredibly nervous, as she had never been in front of a huge audience. For a moment, she thought, *what did I just get myself into?* But then she glanced at Vinya's face, and she thought, *I'm doing this for Vinya.* She got onto the stage with Vinya, and the music started. Vinya started to dance. Sarna followed her cues and started to dance as well. The audience started clapping to the beat. Sarna also started feeling the music and her previous worries dissipated. Some kids even got up and started dancing! Sarna felt so proud of herself. She felt so much energy and happiness. As their performance ended, everyone gave them a standing ovation. It was a new experience for Sarna. This event motivated her to get on stage and face the crowd more. Soon she started to participate in debates and other public activities. Sometimes she would lose competitions, and other times she would win. But she had learned that competitions are there to teach her, rather than just being about winning or losing. Her confidence grew with each competition.

~ *Chapter 6* ~

Sarna was learning so much, and she was having a lot of fun. She would write letters to her parents. She would visit her village every time she got a chance. Initially, her dad would come and take her back home, but as she got older, she started traveling back home on her own. Time flew by and now Sarna was in 10th grade, the last grade in her school. For further studies, she had to get admission in another school that offered grades beyond 10th. But it wasn't free.

During vacations, Sarna went back home. One day she was sitting with her mother on the porch. A thin woman who appeared to be middle-aged passed by her house. It was their neighbor, Jumli. She saw Sarna and stopped.

Jumli asks, "Hey, Sarna's here. How have you been?"

Sarna smiles, "I'm doing alright."

Jumli turns to Sarna's mom, "She's as tall as you, Alaka! It's about time for her to get married, isn't it?"

Sarna's smile grew tight and forced, "I want to study more. I don't want to get married now."

Sarna got up. "I have some work to do. See you." Sarna turned to go inside. Sarna's mom gave Jumli an awkward smile.

Jumli says, "She doesn't understand, but you do, Alaka. If she studies more, it will be hard for you to find a suitor for her. If a woman studies further, it shows they don't pay much attention to their family. Not that Sarna does that..."

Alaka says, "Yes, I understand."

"I don't mean to interfere, of course. I'm just concerned. You shouldn't let this get out of hand. If you want to find her a match, then just let me know."

Alaka says, "Sure. Thanks, Jumli."

Then Jumli leaves. Sarna's mother enters the house.

Sarna looks at her and says, "Why can't people mind their own business here?"

"You know they are our neighbors. They help us out in the times of need. Jumli thinks that getting married is the best thing for you. That's why she is saying that."

"But it's wrong! The best thing for me is to complete my education."

"Yes, Sarna. But how are you going to do that? Your school is only till 10th. What about after that?"

Sarna replies, "I can get admission in a school, in the main city. It is called the J&M

Integrated School and College. But it's not free."

Mother asks, "How much is the fee?"

"I'm not sure. I asked some of my classmates, and they said it's around twenty-five hundred per year."

Mother sat down, "If you're really sure, you'll have to talk to your father about this."

Sarna's father comes back in the evening, after a long day in the fields. Sarna gave him a glass of water. Looking at Sarna's tensed face, Sarna's dad realized that something was bothering her.

Sarna's father asks, "What's the matter, dear?"

Sarna replies, "I want to continue my studies and I've found out that there's a school which I can get admission in, but it's fee is around twenty-five hundred per year. Also, there are no free accommodations. I'll have to pay for my own hostel."

Father replies, "I think, it'll be tight. We can manage to squeeze out the fees for your school. But renting a place in the main city would be costly. We can't afford that."

Sarna was once again in a dilemma. She goes outside and kneels to pray to Mahanguru. *I hope we can figure things out.* She goes to bed, hoping that help would be sent to her once more.

Vacation was over and Sarna went back to her school. She was still thinking about how to solve the problem of admission in the new school. She decided to ask Ms. Kalani about it. Next morning before school, she headed to Ms. Kalani's room. Ms. Kalani seemed surprised to see her this early. She felt that Sarna was really concerned about something.

Ms. Kalani asks, "Is everything alright, Sarna?"

Sarna answers, "Yes. But I wanted to speak with you about something."

Ms. Kalani nodded, "Sure, go ahead."

Sarna explains, "This is my last year here. After the final semester, I'll have to go back to my village. But I want to study more and go to college. I want to go to J&M Integrated School and College."

Ms. Kalani asks, "Have you talked to your family about this yet?"

Sarna replies, "Yes, I did. My father said he would be able to afford the fees for the school, but it'll be hard for him to pay for the accommodation in the main city. I don't think we've got enough money, Ms. Kalani."

Ms. Kalani smiled softly. Knowing the background Sarna was coming from, she was proud to see her wanting to continue her studies.

Ms. Kalani says, "If you don't have enough money, try earning it yourself."

"But how?"

"You can work at a part-time job. You can teach the younger classes here or take tuitions. Also, I've got a friend that works in the local magazine. He was telling me that he wants someone to write some articles for it. You're a great storyteller, so you would be the perfect pick. I could ask him to give you a chance."

Sarna smiles, "Thank you, Ms. Kalani. That would be great! But where should I stay?"

"There are a few students who share a room in my apartment building. Maybe they'd have room for one more. I'll make the arrangements for you."

Sarna smiled. *God has sent help through Ms. Kalani!* She felt very grateful towards her.

Ms. Kalani continues, "After your semester exams are over, ask your father to come here. We can go to J&M and get you admitted."

Sarna says, "Okay, Ms. Kalani. Thank you so much!" She hugged Ms. Kalani and headed back to her class.

~ *Chapter 7* ~

As per Ms. Kalani's plan, Sarna got admitted into J&M Integrated School and College. It was much bigger than her old school. There was a lot to study, and Sarna was enjoying every minute of it. Sarna was also tutoring in a coaching center. She would also go to her old school to teach little children, but that was for free. It was her way of giving back to the school that taught her so much. Her apartment was a few blocks away, a walkable distance from her school. After a hard day at school, she'd come back home and write articles for the local magazine. All this extra work was helping to pay for her accommodation and daily expenses. Her parents would sometimes visit and stay with her as well.

Life was pretty busy for Sarna. One day, she had to write about the local election. She had to research the candidates, their work, and their policies. While she did the research, she learned a lot of new things. She realized that people who run for elections and get elected attain so much power. If they use this power the right way, they can become help sent from God for so many people. She realized the need for good people in politics, and the importance of taking their job seriously.

It was the day of graduation. Sarna's parents had come to attend the ceremony. It was one of the best days of Sarna's life, and it couldn't have been possible without the help of Sarna's parents. To celebrate the occasion, Sarna took them to a restaurant as a treat. Her parents were very happy with Sarna's achievements. She was the most educated person in their entire village. Sarna's dad asks, "What do you want to do next, Sarna?"

Sarna's mom says, "I think you've studied enough. You should think about settling down."

Sarna smiled, "No, now's the time to use what I've learned and enter the workforce. I want to do something that will help other girls like me. How about politics?"

Sarna's parents both looked at each other, then back at Sarna.

Sarna's dad exclaims, "Are you joking?"

Sarna says, "No, I'm serious."

Sarna's dad firmly replies, "No. I know we've supported you, and we've always wanted you to do what you wish. But not politics. We're small people. Sometimes, big people don't like when small people cross their line."

Sarna replies, "I don't want to do that. I just want to work for the people, that's all."

Sarna's mom adds, "You don't understand. They don't consider us as equal. Even us working with them is crossing the line, especially if a woman is doing it."

Sarna was surprised, as this was the first time her parents weren't on the same page as her. But she understood their reactions. *When politicians get elected, they get all sorts of power, which they're supposed to use to help the people. But instead, many times they misuse the power against the same people who helped them get elected.* Sarna didn't try to change their mind. Sarna suggests, "Maybe I'll take some competitive exams for government services, then."

Sarna's mom questions, "And getting married? What about settling down?"

"When the time comes, that will also happen."

Sarna's mom smiled. The food arrived, and they all enjoyed their meal.

~ *Chapter 8* ~

One can feel the anxiousness in the air. Sarna was pacing to-and-fro in her room. Her father was sitting on a rocking chair, newspaper in hand. Her mother came out of the kitchen and said, "What does it say?" Her father puts on his glasses and glances through the series of numbers. He exclaims, "Sarna! You got in! You did it!" Sarna and her mother both started jumping and hugging each other.

Sarna's mother exclaims, "I'm so proud of you!"

Sarna agrees, "I can't believe I got in!"

Sarna's father smiles. "Even if you didn't get in, we'd still be proud. But now that you're an official government employee, it's time to celebrate!"

Sarna says, "Now I can apply for free employee accommodation! I'll have to move to the town where my main office is located."

Sarna got her appointment letter and joined as a government employee in the irrigation department in the state office. Her job involved meeting with local farmers, addressing their problems, and planning and approving projects for their development. She took her job very seriously. She passed many pending projects that involved installation of water pumps, as well as providing free seeds, fertilizer, and financial help to farmers. She supported the women of the region by helping them start small businesses. Her dedication was recognized by everyone in the town.

Time passed, and during that she met the love of her life. She found a loving, caring, and supportive person, named Sajil, who she later married. As the years passed, she had kids. Many times, she had to balance work with her family, but her family was always there to help. She realized that without her family's support, it would be hard to progress in her life. So, she decided she would be the voice for women that weren't as fortunate as her.

~ *Chapter 9* ~

It had been quite some time since she had visited her village. She was very happy with her life, and she was doing a job that let her help people. She was very busy with her work and family, because of which it was not possible for her to visit her old village. So, one day, she planned to visit her village with her husband and kids. When she arrived, she was surprised to see the entire village had come to welcome her. She was the only person that had achieved this much, not to mention the only girl. She was under the impression that since she broke many of the rules her society had, she wouldn't be liked. But to her surprise, everyone seemed to be so proud of her and her accomplishments!

She walked towards her house. She looked around and realized that not much has changed in her village. The roads were still made of dirt, and people were still cooking with firewood. There was only electricity in a few main buildings. Sarna reached home. Her mother was lighting up the oil lantern, as it was getting dark. Her childhood friends, Tilly and Mukul, were also there with their children. Sarna was very happy to see them. It felt like she was going back in time. They all sat down on the porch, watching their kids play.

Sarna asks, "Tilly, your kids are so cute! How old are they?"

Tilly answers, "This is Timki, my oldest. She's twelve. This is Talu, he's eight. And Toba here is five."

"All of your children's names start with T? What's your husband's name?"

Tilly says with a straight face, "Timurku."

Sarna replies, "Oh, that explains it. And what about your family, Mukul?"

Mukul answers, "My kids are ten and five. Our kids play just like how we used to play in the forest. You should move back someday, that way all our kids can play together!"

Sarna laughs, "Maybe someday! Do you send them to school?"

Mukul replies, "Yes. After you, everyone has started sending their kids to school, even the girls!"

Tilly says, "But..."

Sarna repeats, "But what?"

Tilly continues, "But, we only have one school which goes up till 5th grade. Not everyone is willing to send their kids to the main city for studies."

Just then Sarna's mother called, "Dinner is ready! Freshen up and come inside, Sarna!"

Tilly and Mukul said their goodbyes and left. During dinnertime, Sarna kept thinking about the conversation she had with her friends. She was doing so much for the farmers, through her office in town. But she didn't realize the state that her own village was in. The politician that had come to her school long ago, the one she thought was help sent from God, didn't do his job. Not him, nor the other politicians who followed him.

Next morning, she discussed this with her husband, Sajil.

"I want to change this. I want my people to have the basic needs provided to them. I can't just let this happen."

Sarna's husband replies, "I remember you telling me you wanted to get into politics when you graduated."

Sarna nodded.

Sarna's husband asks, "Do you still want to do that?"

"I don't know if I'm capable enough."

"I think you should give it a shot. If you don't do it, who will?"

"Alright, I'll fill up the form for the upcoming election. Let's see what happens."

Sarna was determined to participate in the election. Sarna filed for her candidacy. While she was in the office submitting her form, the person sitting beside her mockingly says, "Hey, that's a first. Do you really think people will vote for a woman? Getting educated is one thing but getting elected as a woman is completely different. Not to mention as a woman from a forest village!" Sarna came out of the office. The comments of that person echoed in her brain, making her question herself. *He's right. What am I doing? I can't do this.* But as she walked, she remembered Tilly and Mukul, and their kids. She realized that whatever she was doing, it was for them. Even if she didn't win, she would be happy that at least she tried.

Sarna had no idea that her work had surpassed the titles that people in society would often attach to her to label her as a weak and incompetent candidate. Titles like her being a woman, her being from a humble background, etc. Now people just know her as a person who takes her work seriously, and actually gets things done. So, of course, she won the election. Now she had the power to make changes, not just for her village, but the entire district.

In the upcoming years, she opened several schools, provided clean drinking water to every household, and brought electricity. She also approved projects to construct new roads and helped people to uplift their financial status. Many times, she faced backlash. But she focused on doing good. Soon her work took her name to the bigger politicians in the state political party. They viewed her as a potential asset to their party, so they offered Sarna to work with them at a state level position. The position they offered her in the party was to be the governor of the state. She accepted. The position gave her even more power. Despite all the power she had, Sarna kept herself grounded and connected to her roots. She worked tirelessly for the people. She was the first woman governor of the state. She won several state and national awards for her good work and spent her entire life working for the people. Sarna was now in her sixties. Her drive to work for the people hadn't faded. By this time, she had enough experience to work for the people at a higher level. Her name was suggested for the topmost position. Everyone in the government accepted her nomination, as her work stood out. And so, she became the president of the nation. Sarna never thought she would become the president. Her big dream was to keep learning and growing. That's all she ever wanted. But for many people in her society, even this much was too much to ask. And despite of all those obstacles, she learned and grew more. And in the process, she understood that she has responsibility toward others. As she gathered more power with her increasing knowledge, she chose to utilize it to create opportunities for others, so they can learn

and grow as well.

~ *Epilogue* ~

A small girl from a small forest village became president of the country. Now, one might think that this only happens in fantasies, but this really happened! Sarna is an imaginary character, but her story has been inspired by a real person's life story. This person is president **Droupadi Murmu.** She is the current president of India, the first one to have a tribal background. She was the first female governor of her state, Jharkhand. Her story is truly inspiring. By pure hard work and dedication, she became the president. This could be anyone in the world who wants to dream big and is willing to work hard for it.

Girls need to be aware of the world around them and understand their capabilities. They need to respect themselves and realize their worth. This can only be possible if they are educated. Sarna's story tells us how important education is. It also emphasizes on the importance of a supportive family. With proper opportunities and support this could be any other girl's story.

As a girl myself, I derive inspiration from President Droupadi Murmu. I hope everyone gets the opportunity to complete their education and follow their dreams. All girls and women must understand their

worth, love themselves, and teach each

other to love, respect, and uplift everyone

around them. –

Gauri.

~ *About the Author* ~

My name is Gauri Subramanian. I love writing short stories and poetry in my free time. I have a little sister, Mira, who loves art and loves to draw and sketch. She illustrated this book! I live in a nice area, with a good school and supportive parents. As a very young kid I used to think that's how everyone's life was more or less, but the truth is far from it. Not everyone is blessed with a loving family or access to affordable education. I wanted to help contribute to the upliftment of people that need this support, so I wrote this book in which all proceeds would go to organizations that work to fund education for underprivileged girls. There are many examples in the world where women have achieved success and happiness despite all the hardships they faced, such as Ruby Bridges and Komako Kimura. Droupadi Murmu is one of them. I feel the need to share the story that inspired me so other girls could derive the courage and strength to face hardships in their lives and so their family understands the importance of encouraging the women in their lives to be confident and independent.

www.ingramcontent.com/pod-product-compliance
Lightning Source LLC
Chambersburg PA
CBHW050824250726
48653CB00006B/2416